BEING BORN AGAIN

A STUDY OF
THE "BORN AGAIN" EXPERIENCE

JOHN MARINELLI

TABLE OF CONTENTS

Preface v

Introduction vii

Chapter One: What Does Being,
"Born Again" Mean"? 1

Chapter Two: Why should I be
"Born Again"? 7

Chapter Three: Why Do People
Reject Being "Born Again"? 11

Chapter Four: Depravity And The
New Birth Experience 15

Chapter Five: The "New Creature"
And The "New Birth." 37

Conclusion 41

Selected Christian Poetry By
John Marinelli, The Author 45

About The Author 65

PREFACE

Many folks do not know what it means to be "Born Again." Even Christians are at a loss to describe the "Born Again" experience, much less admit that they have experienced it.

My book reveals the Biblical truths about being "Born Again." We will discuss the need for it; the process, the benefits; the Biblical proof text; the overall statistics of Christianity, and some other aspects of the experience.

I will use the King James Version of the Bible as a support reference and other generally accepted Internet references that may add to the overall discussion.

INTRODUCTION

Christianity is the largest religion in the United States. Over the past 50 years, there has been a steady decline in total numbers from 83% to 65%. Here are a few statistics from the Pew Research Center that track trends in religion and many other aspects of American life.

A Profile of An American Christian

45% are men and 55% are women; 66% are white; 77% are 3rd generation; 76% expressed a belief in God; 47% attend church at least once per week; 68% pray regularly; 47% do not take part in Bible studies; 45% meditate weekly; 65% feel a sense of peace at least once a week; 43% look to religion as a source of right and wrong; 59% feel that right and wrong depends on the situation; 45% read the scriptures at least once a week; 39% believe the "Word of God" should be taken literally while 33% do not.

85% believe in heaven; 70% believe in hell; 43% are

Republican and 40% Democrat; 44% Conservative; 51% say abortion should be illegal and 45% say it should be legal; 54% say homosexuality should be accepted and 38% say it should be discouraged; 44% strongly favor same-sex marriages among Christians and 48% strongly oppose it; 29% favor evolution as God's creation design and 42% say man was always in this present form;

In 1970, 90% of Americans identified themselves as Christian. In 2010, the percentage dropped to 71%.

In the United States, approximately 63% of the population, which translates to around 210 million people, identify as Christian. This includes various Christian denominations, religious groups, and traditions.

Interestingly, the percentage of Christians has been gradually declining over the years. In 2018 and 2019, about 65% of American adults identified as Christians, which corresponds to roughly 167 million individuals. This decline reflects changing religious landscapes and diverse beliefs among individuals in the country.

In 2023, people who identified as Christian totaled 70.6 %. However, there was a significant decline in adults, from 78% in 2007 to 63% currently. (Pew Research Center)

Note: It is crucial to understand that the above study encompasses all individuals who identify as Christian, including Gays, liberals, Mormons, and other segments that may or may believe in Jesus. Some will even deny the deity of Christ yet call themselves Christian. The foundation of the Christian faith is a relationship with Christ, not a religion. We will see why this is so important as we read the upcoming chapters.

Here is what I see in the statistics:

- There is a steady decline in Christian adult believers.

- Les and les read and study the Bible.

- Over 50% do not attend any church.

- Situational ethics is more prevalent than ever, destroying absolute Biblical truth.

- Homosexuality, a Biblical sin against God and man, is more accepted than ever before.

- More and more Christians believe in evolution as God's plan for creation which is against the Biblical account of creation as recorded in Genesis.

- More of today's Christian community accepts same-sex marriages among Christians.

- Many have fallen away from the faith to follow false doctrine and teachings.

Forty-five percent of Americans say they have a personal commitment to Jesus Christ, have confessed their sins, and accepted Christ as Savior according to The Barna Group. But even survey author George Barna agrees that not all born-again Christians are bearing fruit. What we are finding is that there is still a lot of superficiality related to the fact that a lot of people have recognized that the spiritual dimension of their life is important. Barna finds that 36 percent of Americans are what he calls *NOTION-AL Christians*, they describe themselves as Christians but do not meet the born-again definition.

My question is, if there is a steady decline in adult Christians and only 45% say they are "Born Again", what is the experience all about that so many refuse to be "Born Again?" If most Christians are not "Born Again" why not?

CHAPTER ONE:
WHAT DOES BEING, "BORN AGAIN" MEAN"?

Here is what the dictionary says:

born-a·gain…[ˌbôrnəˈgen]

ADJECTIVE… (of a person) converted to a personal faith in Christ (with reference to John 3:3): *"a born-again Christian"*

Being "Born Again" is a spiritual transformation that occurs when a person embraces faith in Jesus Christ. Here are the key aspects:

- **Spiritual Rebirth**:
  - It is not about physical birth but about a new beginning in one's relationship with God.
  - Through faith, a believer experiences a regeneration of the human spirit.

- The soul is renewed, and the power of sin is broken.
- **Biblical Basis**:
  - Jesus introduced the concept in a conversation with Nicodemus (John 3:3-4).
  - Jesus emphasized that being "Born Again" is essential for seeing the kingdom of God.
  - It is a spiritual birth, not a physical one.
- **Grace and Righteousness**:
  - Humans are judged under the law, but God's grace offers a way out.
  - Faith in Jesus leads to forgiveness of sins and imputed righteousness.
  - Romans 6:4 speaks of being buried with Christ and raised to new life.
- **God's Grace and Judgment:**
  - Sin affects the soul, but when faith is placed in Jesus, the soul is renewed.
  - Without God's grace, humans face judgment under the law.

Being "Born Again" is God's way of granting new life and salvation to those who believe (Copilot- AI Explanation)

Being "Born Again" is about embracing God's grace, receiving forgiveness, and entering a new life in Christ.

The phrase translated "Born Again" can also be translated as "born from above." Nicodemus had a real need. He needed a change of his heart—a spiritual transformation that could only come from above. New birth, being "Born Again", is an act of God whereby eternal life is imparted to the person who believes (2 Corinthians 5:17; Titus 3:5; 1 Peter 1:3; 1 John 2:29; 3:9; 4:7; 5:1–4, 18). John 1:12–13 indicates that being "Born Again" also carries the idea of becoming "children of God" through trust in the name of Jesus Christ.

The question logically comes, "Why does a person need to be born again?" The apostle Paul in Ephesians 2:1 says, "And you he made alive, who were dead in trespasses and sins" (NKJV). To the Romans he wrote, "For all have sinned and fall short of the glory of God" (Romans 3:23). Sinners are spiritually "dead"; when they receive spiritual life through faith in Christ, the Bible likens it to a rebirth. Only those who are "Born Again" have their sins forgiven and have a relationship with God.

Twice in his conversation with Nicodemus, Jesus stressed the truth that one must be "Born Again" to enter the kingdom of God (John 3:3, 5). Being born *once* makes us children of Adam, and we share Adam's corruption. We need a *second* birth—a spiritual birth—to make us children of God. We must be "Born again."

The classic passage from the Bible that answers this question is John 3:1–21. The Lord Jesus Christ is talking to

Nicodemus, a prominent Pharisee and member of the Sanhedrin (the ruling body of the Jews). Nicodemus had come to Jesus at night with some questions. Jesus told him he must be "Born Again"

There is a metaphor seen in nature that depicts this experience. It is the story of the Butterfly. As you may know, the butterfly undergoes a miraculous transformation from a caterpillar into an entirely new creature. So it is with the human soul. It undergoes a transformation from unrighteous and evil to righteous; from darkness to light; from death to life.

I wrote this poem a while back. I think it tells the story as it depicts man as a butterfly.

Be A Butterfly

Be a Butterfly
And fly away with me.
We'll fly on God's Promises
Right into eternity.
Be a Butterfly
To crawl no more.
But to soar in the Spirit
Above earth's mighty roar.
Be a Butterfly
To fly to heights unknown.
Soaring on the wings of faith
Never more to be alone.
Be a Butterfly
And fly away with me.
For God has made us new
At last! At last! We are free

CHAPTER TWO:
WHY SHOULD I BE "BORN AGAIN"?

Why should I be "Born Again?" After all, over 50% of American Christians are not. They go to church and even practice their religion faithfully. They are, for the most part, good people.

Paul tells us in his letter to the Roman Christians in the 1st century what went wrong and how to fix it. He said, (Romans 5:12 ,14,17 & 21)

"Wherefore, as by one man sin entered into the world, and death by sin; and so death passed upon all men, for that all have sinned: (5:14) (For until the law sin was in the world: but sin is not imputed when there is no law.

Nevertheless, death reigned from Adam to Moses, even over them that had not sinned after the similitude of Adam's transgression, who is the figure of him that was to come. (5:17)

For if by one man's offence death reigned by one; much more they which receive abundance of grace and of the gift of righteousness shall reign in life by one, Jesus Christ.) (5:21) That as sin hath reigned unto death, even so might grace reign through righteousness unto eternal life by Jesus Christ our Lord."

I should be "Born Again" so I can become the new creature God has planned for me; so I can become a "Child of God"; so I can dwell in his presence for all eternity; so I can finally be free from the sin that plagues my soul day and night; so I can fellowship with my Heavenly Father.

The main reason for us to be "Born Again" is because it is our divine destiny. It is the will of God. It is the only way we will see heaven, Jesus and all the saints. This is the pathway to God, the Father. Here are some other benefits. (taken from the AI CoPilot):

Being "**Born Again**" holds significant spiritual and personal benefits for believers. Let us explore some of these:

- **Salvation And Eternal Life**: The primary benefit is **salvation**. When a person is "Born Again" through faith in Jesus Christ, they receive forgiveness for their sins and the promise of **eternal life**. This new birth marks the beginning of a transformed life and relationship with God.

- **Spiritual Transformation**: Being "Born Again" involves a **spiritual rebirth**. The

Holy Spirit indwells the believer, empowering him to live a life that reflects God's character. Old habits and sinful patterns are replaced by new desires and godly attitudes. (over time)

- **New Identity**: Through the new birth, believers receive a **new identity**. They become "Children of God", adopted into his family. Their status changes from being spiritually dead to being alive in Christ.

- **Freedom From Bondage**: "Born Again" believers experience freedom from the bondage of sin. The power of sin is broken, and they can overcome temptations through the Holy Spirit's guidance.

- **Purpose And Calling**: God has a unique purpose for each believer. Being "Born Again" opens the door to discovering and fulfilling that purpose. Believers are called to serve God and others, using their gifts and talents for his glory.

- **Assurance of God's Love**: The new birth assures believers of God's unwavering love. They know that nothing can separate them from his love (Romans 8:38-39).

- **Fellowship With Other Believers**: "Born Again" Christians become part of the global family of believers. They find fellowship, encouragement, and support from other followers of Jesus.

- **Hope And Joy**: The hope of eternal life and the joy of knowing Christ bring deep satisfaction. Born Again" believers experience a sense of purpose and fulfillment that transcends earthly circumstances.

Remember that being "Born Again" is not a mere ritual; it is a profound transformation of the heart and soul. Jesus emphasized this truth when he said, "Truly, truly, I say to you, unless one is born again, he cannot see the kingdom of God" (John 3:3, ESV). It is an invitation to experience God's grace and enter a new life in Christ.

CHAPTER THREE:

WHY DO PEOPLE REJECT BEING "BORN AGAIN"?

Being "Born Again" begins with God. He draws us to himself. (John 6:44) Jesus declares that "no one can come to me unless the Father who sent me draws him, and I will raise him up at the last day."

However, the call to salvation is an open invitation to all who believe. John 3:16 tells us, **"For God so loved the world, that he gave his only begotten Son, that whosoever believeth in him should not perish, but have everlasting life." The whosoever is called. God is no respecter of persons. He calls everyone, and those who believe in Christ as his only begotten Son find salvation in Jesus.**

People reject the concept of being "Born Again" for various reasons, and these can be deeply personal. Here are some common reasons:

- **Misunderstanding or Lack of Awareness:**

Some individuals may not fully understand what it means to be "Born Again." They might associate it with religious rituals or legalistic requirements rather than a genuine spiritual transformation.

- **Intellectual Skepticism**: People with a skeptical mindset may question the idea of spiritual rebirth. They might find it difficult to accept supernatural concepts without empirical evidence.

- **Fear of Change**: Being "Born Again" implies a radical shift in one's life. It requires surrendering control and embracing God's plan. Some people fear this change and prefer to remain in their own comfort zone

- **Negative Experiences With Religion**: Past negative experiences within religious institutions or with religious leaders can lead to rejection. Hurtful encounters, hypocrisy, or legalism can create a barrier to accepting spiritual truths.

- **Worldly Attachments**: Materialism, worldly desires, and attachments can hinder openness to spiritual matters. The pursuit of pleasure, success, or self-centered goals may overshadow the need for spiritual rebirth.

- **Pride and Self-Reliance**: Pride can prevent someone from acknowledging their need for salvation. Believing they can achieve righteousness on their own, they reject the idea of being "Born Again" through faith in Christ.

- **Moral Relativism**: In a culture that promotes moral relativism, some people reject absolute truth. They may view the concept of being "Born Again" as narrow-minded.

- **Emotional Barriers**: Past trauma, emotional wounds, or unresolved issues can create emotional barriers. Accepting spiritual rebirth may require addressing these underlying hurts.

- **Peer Pressure And Social Acceptance**: Fear of rejection by peers or society can influence a person's decision. Choosing to be "Born Again" may set them apart from their social circles.

- **No Real Kneed**: The belief that all people of this world are already "Children of God." Thus, there is no need for a new birth.

- **Spiritual Warfare**: The Bible speaks of spiritual forces opposing God's truth. These unseen battles can influence a person's receptivity to the gospel message.

It is essential to approach these reasons with empathy and understanding. Encouraging open dialogue and sharing personal testimonies can help bridge the gap and lead people toward the transformative experience of being "Born Again." (Excerpts from Odyssey)

As I see it, ***the major reason*** folks reject being "Born Again" is that they do not believe in the fall of man from God's grace. Romans 5:12 clearly shows what happened. It says, "Wherefore, as by one man sin entered into the world, and death by sin; and so death passed upon all men, for that all have sinned"

Sin entered the world by the disobedience of Adam and passed on to his descendants. The sin was a willful rejection of God and his divine will…an attitude of rebellion that caused every descendent of Adam to also sin. No one could escape this evil nature that came from Adam. Thus, people reject being "Born Again" because they are in a state of rebellion all the time and care not about God's grace. They are too busy being their own god.

CHAPTER FOUR:
DEPRAVITY AND THE NEW BIRTH EXPERIENCE

It is true that man is totally depraved and cannot seek after God. It is also true that God seeks after man with his grace to offer redemption. Critics have suggested that man cannot respond because of his total depravity. That is foolish, in my opinion. Is God all powerful? Can he not speak to the dead soul and call it back to live or give it life?

Here is how I see things…God chose the elect before the foundation of the world. That choice was based upon his foreknowledge. Being always everywhere, he can see who will believe and who will not. He did not select some for salvation and damn others to hell. He extended the salvation call to everyone. (See John 3:16) Then see Romans 8:29-30. Those who believed were called, justified, and glorified. They were pre-selected to have a destination which was to be like Jesus. That is what predestination is all about. Depravity did not stop the will of God to redeem humanity.

Now, let us look at some new thoughts and do some review so we stay on the same page. **Here is what Jesus said**.

"Jesus answered and said unto him, Verily, verily, I say unto thee, except a man be born again, he cannot see the kingdom of God." John 3:3

The Pew report tells us that there are a large percentage of evangelicals that do not identify themselves as, "Born Again." What happens to these folks? Is there a different place that they will go when they die? According to Jesus, to see the kingdom of God, you must be "Born Again."

We know from the rest of the scriptures that there is a heaven, a kingdom of God, and there is a hell. (a place of torment). It is heaven or hell. Some will benefit and some will not. Could it be that 51% of all Methodists, 55% of all Presbyterians, 63% of all Lutherans, 29% of all Adventists and 29% of all Restorationists will not see the kingdom of God?

The Pew Research Center reports that 15 % of all Evangelicals and 21% of all nondenominational Christians do not identify themselves as," Born Again" This report also says that 78% of all Catholics do not identify themselves as being," Born Again".

Deception Rules The Day

According to the latest survey conducted by the Pew

Forum on Religion and Public Life, sixty-five percent of all Christians say there are multiple paths to eternal life, ultimately rejecting the exclusivity of Christ as the only way.

Even among white evangelical Protestants, 72 percent of those who say many religions can lead to eternal life name at least one non-Christian religion, such as Islam or no religion at all, that can lead to salvation.

Dr. R. Albert Mohler, Jr., president of the Southern Baptist Theological Seminary, called the survey results "a theological crisis for American evangelicals," according to USA Today.

Majorities among white Evangelicals, white Mainline Christians, and Black Protestants who do not believe in the exclusivity of salvation say Catholicism and Judaism can lead to eternal life, Pew results show.

Smaller but still sizeable percentages (more than half) of white mainline Christians, black Protestants and white Catholics who say there are multiple ways to eternal life also say Islam can lead to salvation; among white evangelicals, 35 percent agree. And more than half of white mainline Christians and white Catholics who view heaven's gates as wide say Hinduism can lead to eternal life compared to 33 percent of white evangelicals and 44 percent of black Protestants.

Surprisingly, Christians also believe atheism can provide

a ticket to heaven. Forty-six percent of white mainline Christians, 49 percent of white Catholics and 26 percent of white evangelicals who believe many religions lead to salvation say atheism can lead to eternal life. (Researchers conducted this study several years ago.)

Mohler called the findings "an indictment of evangelicalism and evangelical preaching."

The Bible Tells The Truth

These folks that view the path to heaven as wide go against Biblical truth. Here is what the Bible says:

Neither is there salvation in any other: for there is none other name under heaven given among men, whereby we must be saved. Acts 4:12

Jesus saith unto him, I am the way, the truth, and the life: no man comes unto the Father, but by me. John 14:6

I am the door: by me if any man enter in, he shall be saved, and shall go in and out, and find pasture. John 10:9

Behold, I stand at the door, and knock: if any man hear my voice, and open the door, I will come in to him, and will sup with him, and he with me. Revelation 3:20

Jesus said, "Enter ye in at the strait gate: for wide *is* the gate, and broad *is* the way, that leads to destruction, and many there be which go in thereat: Because strait *is* the gate, and narrow *is* the way, which leads unto life, and few there be that find it. Matthew 7:13-14

It hurts me to read about how many people who claim to be Christian deceive themselves and follow the wrong path in life. I guess they believe that their church will save them or their good works or the fact that they are worthy in some other way to qualify for eternal life.

Before we deal with depravity and how to be "Born Again" …to experience a new or 2nd birth, it is important to look at why it is necessary and why Jesus is the only one that can get us to heaven.

Just "One" Way?

It is hard for most folks that are not "Born Again" to understand why there is just one way to God, yet it is true. There is only one way and that is through Jesus Christ. The Bible is our source to prove that the one-way doctrine is valid. Acts 4:12 says, "Neither is there salvation in any other: for there is none other name under heaven given among men, whereby we must be saved." (I referred to this scripture several times.)

Here is why it is so important. Adam sinned against God and died spiritually. "And the LORD God commanded the man, saying, of every tree of the garden thou may freely eat: But of the tree of the knowledge of good and evil, thou shalt not eat of it: for in the day that thou eat thereof ***thou shalt surely die***." Genesis 2:16-17

This creation account shows him being made of clay and God breathing into him the breath of life. He thus became a living soul. "And the LORD God formed man of the dust of the ground, and breathed into his nostrils the breath of life; and man became a living soul." Genesis 2:7. When he sinned, he lost the breath of life, and he became a dead soul. He was truly the first of a race which became, "The Walking Dead".

Life is always in relationship to God. It is his breath or Spirit that makes us alive. So, death passed upon all men for all sinned. (Romans 5:12) Their nature was now sinful. We see this in all of us and in our society.

The 2nd birth experience is by the Spirit. The Spirit gives the "Breath of God" to each repentant heart and awakens their souls to God. They become his children by birth.

Jesus is the only way to attain salvation. All the world religions cannot save us. Joining a church or specific faith cannot save us. It must be an acknowledgment of our sin, our repentant heart's cry before the throne of God for forgiveness, and our invitation to Jesus to come into our hearts and save us. His name is the only name that can get us through death into eternal life.

Here are a few scriptures that support the "One-Way" doctrine.

...There is one God, and one mediator between God and men, the man Christ Jesus; Who gave himself a ransom for all, to be testified in due time. (I Timothy 2:5-6)

...Believe on the Lord Jesus Christ and thou shalt be saved... (Acts 16:31)

That if thou shalt confess with thy mouth the Lord Jesus, and shalt believe in thine heart that God hath raised him from the dead, *THOU SHALT BE SAVED*. For with the heart man believes unto righteousness; and with the mouth confession is made unto salvation. (Romans 10:9-10)

The skeptic would say," You mean to tell me that all the religions of the world are wrong and only Christianity is the one true religion?" Remember, Christianity is not a religion. It is a relationship born out of love between man and the one true and living God. There is no one true religion. Religion will not get us to God. It is the blood of Christ that unlocks the door and our confession of faith in Jesus that makes it all happen. (John 14:6)

Why is Jesus the only way to God? ...Because God planned it that way. He set the penalty for sin, which was death. The soul that sins, it shall die. (Ezekiel 18:20) In fact, Jesus was the slain Lamb of God before the foundation of the world. (Ephesians 1:3-7)

Jesus himself said, as recorded in John 14:6, "I am the way, the truth, and the life: No man comes to the Father but by me". Christianity states that the God of the Bible is the only true God and salvation is only possible by accepting Jesus Christ, his only begotten Son as Savior and Lord. II Corinthians 5:21 says, "For he hath made him to be sin for us, who knew no sin; that we might be made the righteousness of God in him."

Validation

God validated his Son as the only way in multiple ways so we could be assured that Jesus was indeed the only way to him. Here are some to consider.

- He claimed to be the only way as in John's record 14:6 says but validation came through miracles that proved he was who he claimed to be.

- Eyewitnesses saw Jesus' miracles and validated them as authentic. Over 500 followers saw Jesus, after his resurrection, and watched him ascend into heaven.

- The prophets foretold of his coming, where he would be born, that he would be God in human flesh and lots more…all prophetic statements were realized in Jesus, even those like in Isaiah chapter 53 that were uttered hundreds of years before Jesus came.

- God himself validated Jesus as his sole pathway to him. "While he was still speaking, behold, a bright cloud overshadowed them; and suddenly a voice came out of the cloud, saying, "This is My Beloved Son, in whom I am well pleased. Hear ye him!" (Mathew 17:5)

- The apostles lost their homes, wealth, and even their lives preaching the gospel. Would they do that if it were a lie? I don't think so. They testified to the truth and were willing to die for it if necessary. (Read Foxes Book of Martyrs)

- Thousands of Believers, over several centuries have testified of how Jesus helped them and blessed them.

- I can personally testify that I have seen the hand of the Lord in my life and communicate with him daily. I know he is the Christ.

The provability that one man could fulfill all prophecies about a Messiah that God himself said would come, (Gen.3:15), and perform fantastic miracles while here on earth, and be raised from the dead, and ascend into heaven while hundreds looked on is astronomical. But Jesus did just that…fulfilled everything that was foretold about the coming Messiah. He had to be who he said he was and therefore is truly the only way to God.

How To Be Born Again

It should be obvious by now that it is essential for anyone who wants eternal life to be, "Born Again." Romans 10:9-10 will tell us how.

"That if thou shalt confess with thy mouth the Lord Jesus, and shalt believe in thine heart that God hath raised him from the dead, thou shalt be saved. For with the heart man believes unto righteousness; and with the mouth confession is made unto salvation." Romans 10:9-10

Confessing Jesus is to acknowledge his Lordship and openly proclaim your allegiance. There is no secret society. That is why the scripture says, "With Thy Mouth."

Believing with the heart is different than with the mind. When we believe with our heart, it means to rely upon, adhere to and trust in. We are to wholly embrace the truth that God raised up Jesus from the dead after being crucified for the sins of mankind.

The power to save us and birth us into his kingdom as his child is in the fact that our heartfelt belief brings us the righteousness of Christ and our open mouth of continual confession in him as our savior actually saves us. It is not all God, nor is it all man. It is an invitation and a favorable response.

Remember what Paul wrote to the Romans in Romans chapter five? He said, in effect, that Adam was the 1st man who fell into sin and took the entire race with him. Thus, death passed upon all of us. However, Jesus was the 2nd Adam or last man that was sent outside of the pollution of human sinful DNA via a "Virgin Birth" to be the spotless Lamb of God and to be slain as a sacrifice for sin to abolish it forever. This is why the "New Birth" is necessary, to free us from the sin of the 1st Adam and propel us by spiritual birth into the kingdom of God.

How Do We Know For Sure?

"The Spirit itself bears witness with our spirit, that we are the children of God: And if children, then heirs; heirs of God, and joint-heirs with Christ; if so be that we suffer with him, that we may be also glorified together." Romans 8:15-17

We who have believed can say that we are his children, without a doubt or any question in our minds. We can because the Spirit of God is continually bearing witness with our spirits. He leads us; he communicates with us; he teaches us and shows us truth and error. That's how we know for sure.

If you have never seen the hand of God in your life or heard the spirit speaking to you, you might want to go back to God and repent of your sins, ask his forgiveness, and ask Jesus to come into your heart and save you. Then receive Jesus as your Lord. This is the only way you can be "Born Again."

How Does This Experience Change Us

"And you were dead in your trespasses and sins, in which you formerly walked according to the course of this world, according to the prince of the power of the air, of the spirit that is now working in the sons of disobedience. Among them we too all formerly lived in the lusts of our flesh, indulging the desires of the flesh and of the mind, and were by nature children of wrath, even as the rest.

But God, being rich in mercy, because of his great love with which he loved us, even when we were dead in our transgressions, made us alive together with Christ (by grace you have been saved), and raised us up with him, and seated us with Him in the heavenly *places* in Christ Jesus, so that in the ages to come he might show the surpassing riches of his grace in kindness toward us in Christ Jesus.

For by grace, you have been saved through faith; and that not of yourselves, *it is* the gift of God; not as a result of works, so that no one may boast. For we are his workmanship, created in Christ Jesus for good works, which God prepared beforehand so that we would walk in them. Remember that you were at that time separate from Christ, excluded from the commonwealth of Israel, and strangers to the covenants of promise, having no hope and without God in the world.

But now in Christ Jesus you who formerly were far off

have been brought near by the blood of Christ. For he himself is our peace, who made both groups into one and broke down the barrier of the dividing wall, by abolishing in his flesh the enmity, which is the Law of commandments contained in ordinances, so that in himself he might make the two into one new man, thus establishing peace, and might reconcile them both in one body to God through the cross, by it having put to death the enmity.

And he came and preached peace to you who were far away, and peace to those who were near; for through him we both have our access in one Spirit to the Father.

So then, you are no longer strangers and aliens, but you are fellow citizens with the saints, and are of God's household, having been built on the foundation of the apostles and prophets, Christ Jesus himself being the corner stone, in whom the whole building, being fitted together, is growing into a holy temple in the Lord, in whom you also are being built together into a dwelling of God in the Spirit." Ephesians 2:1-22 ASV

Read this again. It tells you where you were or are now and where God takes you when you are "Born Again." It is truly a life changing experience.

More Benefits of The New Birth

There are ten more benefits that overtake the believer at his new birth. They are:

- We experience God's great Mercy and Love.

- We are made alive to God, given eternal life.

- We were raised up with Christ and seated with him in Heavenly Places.

- We receive his Grace or unmerited favor.

- We are brought close to God by the Blood of Christ.

- Jesus becomes our peace.

- We gain access to God through his Spirit.

- We are no longer strangers but fellow citizens and joint heirs with Christ.

- We are becoming a spiritual dwelling for God.

- We are his workmanship, created in Christ Jesus unto good works that were established before we were saved so we could walk in them.

We have looked at statistics that show trends and percentages of those in error. We have discussed doctrines like Jesus as the only pathway to God, The Father. We have looked at benefits of being "Born Again" and why it is necessary to attain eternal life. We have seen how to be "Born Again" through repentance, a plea for forgiveness and an invitation to Jesus to enter our hearts and be Lord over our lives.

There is only one thing left to do, decide if you are, "Born

Again" or not. If not, go before the Lord and ask to be born into his kingdom. Then follow the teachings of Jesus.

Now, let us look deeper into this depravity so we are clear on the subject related to being saved. I say this because there is a hugh split in the church over eternal security and being saved. Some say, it is all of God and man has no free will to accept or choose God's call, unless he or she was chosen before the world began. Others will reject that premise and say we do have the power of choice and can accept or reject God's call to salvation.

The ***Sovereignty of God*** is the theological assumption. It says that all things are under God's rule and control and that nothing happens without his direction. God works, not just some things, but all things, according to the counsel of his own will (see Eph. 1:11). His purposes are all-inclusive and never thwarted (see Isa. 46:11); nothing takes him by surprise. The sovereignty of God is not merely that God has the power to govern all things, but that he does so, always and without exception. God is not merely sovereign in principle, but also sovereign in practice.

"Although the sovereignty of God is universal and absolute, it is not the sovereignty of blind power. Coupled with infinite wisdom, holiness, and love, sovereignty embodies a universal and absolute power. And this doctrine, when properly understood, is most comforting. Who would not prefer his or her affairs to be in the hands of a God of infinite power, wisdom, holiness, and love?

The alternative is to have them left to fate, chance, or irrevocable natural law, or to shortsighted and perverted self. Those who reject God's sovereignty should consider what alternatives they have left." (Loraine Boettner, author of Reformed Doctrine of Predestination.)

God created all beings, including the angels, but some have fallen. Let us be sure that this does not make God the author of sin, for, as man, they fell from their created state. This includes all false gods. But God is over them, whether they be angels, demons, or the devil.

A man may fight against God, but he cannot win. God often uses evil men to accomplish his will in battle. Jesus is said to have been slain from the foundation of the world, and the cross is one of the most credible pieces of evidence of God's sovereignty.

"Crucify him," "Crucify him", was their cry, but when they nailed him to the cross, they did not realize they were fulfilling God's will for his Son. Peter said, "him (Christ), being delivered by the determinate counsel and foreknowledge of God, ye have taken and by wicked hands have crucified and slain." Acts 2:23. But this God of all power was not defeated in this evil act, for the Lord Jesus was raised from the dead. By it, the devil was defeated and all his ministers of (self) righteousness. This is a great example of God's sovereignty in action.

The Psalmist said, *"Thou are exalted far above all gods,"* Psalm 97:9, And again, *"Our Lord is above all gods,"* Psalm 135.5, *"O give thanks unto the God of gods."* Psalm 136.2.

Our God cannot fail, lie, or sin. Neither is he frustrated at man's failure. God is the author of his sovereign grace and mercy.

"For he saith to Moses, I will have mercy on whom I will have mercy, and I will have compassion on whom I will have compassion. So, it is not of him that wills, nor of him that runs, but of God that shows mercy... And whom he will, he hardens." (Rom. 9:15-16, 18.)

Judas, who betrayed Jesus, had betrayed himself and met his just due. John wrote, "Jesus knew from the beginning who should betray him. And he said,

"No man can come unto me, except it were given unto him of my Father ... Have not I chosen you twelve, and one of you is a devil (i.e., slanderer) ... He spoke of Judas ... for he it was that should betray him, being one of the twelve." (John 6:64-71.)

Many Christians have doubts about God's sovereignty. Yet there is one aspect of the Christian life where they profess, maybe unknowingly, that God is sovereign. They said as many do, "God has done all he can do. Now the rest is up to you."

How contradictory! They may stand on their feet and deny this blessed, comforting, enabling doctrine, but when they bend their knees in prayer, asking God to save them, do they not realize they are calling on a sovereign God, whom only he has the right and the ability to save?

The question is, If God has done all that he can do, why pray to him? But we pray knowing he is the only one who can do what man cannot otherwise do. This power belongs to God, and not man. (Excerpts from Sovereign Grace Baptist Proclaimer)

The current doctrine of sovereignty emerged over five centuries ago. It is the Protestant theological system that fosters predestination. Calvinism, as the doctrine is called, was the theology of John Calvin, a French theologian and Protestant reformer in the 16th century.

Those who follow this "Predestination" theology believe that God, in his sovereign rule, saved some of humanity and damned the rest. They are commonly known as "Hyper-Calvinists." Their viewpoint includes justification by faith alone, with emphasis on the grace of God. The doctrine of predestination, which holds that God has already determined who will be saved and who will be damned, is a key tenet of John Calvin's teachings.

Calvinism has had a significant impact on the development of Western culture and has influenced many aspects of modern society. (*I believe that this teaching is heresy and should be discarded as error.*)

This acrostic will help us remember the Calvinistic

doctrine, TULIP. Check out my book titled, "***It's Your Choice, or Is It***" for a complete review of both Calvinism and Arminianism (Free Will) in relationship to the Sovereignty of God.

- T- Total depravity
- U- Unconditional Election
- L- Limited Atonement
- Irresistible Grace
- P- Perseverance of the saints

It is important to know this stuff. Most of the Protestant movement is based upon it. Most folks cannot quote the TULIP acrostic, but they believe and practice it just the same. Here is a description of the first letter of the acrostic.

Total Depravity…means complete, not partial. It is total. When someone is depraved, they live in a quality or state that is corrupt or perverted. Here are some synonyms of depravity: abjection, corruption, corruptness, debasement, debauchery, decadence, decadency, degeneracy, degenerateness, degeneration, degradation, demoralization, dissipatedness, dissipation, dissoluteness, libertinage, libertinism, perversion, perverseness, rakishness, and turpitude.

From the Christian perspective, depravity means sin, sinfulness, unrighteous, ungodly, and evil.

Note: The teaching says there is no escape from this state of being. It is total and complete in every form. We cannot just do or get better on our own. The condition is permanent and final. It came to us through Adam and his fall from grace. (See Romans 5:12) (***God is greater than depravity, total or partial.***)

The implications of "Total Depravity" are:

- We can do good works, but they will not change the underlying condition of depravity. "As it is written: "There is none righteous, no, not one; There is none who understands; There is none who seeks after God. They have all turned aside; They have all together become unprofitable; There is none who does good, no, not one." Romans 3:10.

- We can try to be good and even claim to be righteous, but that will not make us better. "The heart *is* deceitful above all things and desperately wicked: who can know it?" Jeremiah 17:9.

- Man's righteousness misses the mark. Isaiah 64:6 said, "all our righteousness is like filthy rags." The Pharisees had righteousness, but Jesus asserts that our righteousness must exceed theirs (Matthew 5:20), meaning that we need to have his righteousness imputed to us, which becomes our new covering, our new garment.

- We were born dead, dead to God, and lost. "And you hath he quickened, who were dead in trespasses and sins; Wherein in time past ye walked according to the course of this world, according to the prince of the power of the air, the spirit that now works in the children of disobedience: Among whom also we all had our conversation in times past in the lusts of our flesh, fulfilling the desires of the flesh and the mind; and were by nature the children of wrath, even as others. But God, who is rich in mercy, for his great love wherewith he loved us, even when we were dead in sins, hath quickened us together with Christ, (by grace ye are saved;) And hath raised us up together, and made us sit together in heavenly places in Christ Jesus." Ephesians 2:1-7.

I believe that man has a "free will" that God gave him and he does exercise it liberally. God has the power to speak to the dead and call them back to life. He can surely call the spiritually dead to salvation. He is greater than man's depravity.

Note: God does not damn anyone, nor does he select billions to spend an eternity in hell. People make free will choices that take them to eternal destruction.

Being "Born Again" is an experience that shows the call of God into the deadness of man and the response of those who accept. They are the "Whosoevers" of John 3:16 Man does have a say-so in being born again and being a child of God. It's all about God's call to salvation and man's response. The "Born Again" folks accepted the invitation while the damned rejected it.

If you are not born again, you should be. Your eternal destiny hangs in the balance.

CHAPTER FIVE:
THE "NEW CREATURE"
AND THE "NEW BIRTH."

The new creation is described in 2 Corinthians 5:17: *"Therefore, if anyone is in Christ, he is a new creation; the old has gone, the new has come!"*

The word "therefore" refers us back to verses 14-16 where Paul tells us that all believers have died with Christ and no longer live for themselves. Our lives are no longer worldly; they are now spiritual. Our "death" is that of the old sin nature which was nailed to the cross with Christ. It was buried with him, and just as he was raised up by the Father, so are we raised up to "walk in newness of life" (Romans 6:4). That new person that was raised up is what Paul refers to in 2 Corinthians 5:17 as the "New Creation."

To understand the new creation, first we must grasp that it is in fact a creation, something created by God. John 1:13 tells us that this new birth was brought about by the will of God. We did not inherit the new nature from our parents or decide to re-create ourselves anew. Neither did God simply clean up our old nature; He created something entirely fresh and unique. The "New Creation" is completely new, brought about from nothing, just as the whole universe was created by God ex nihilo, from nothing. Only the Creator could accomplish such a feat.

"Old things have passed away." The "old" refers to everything that is part of our old nature—natural pride, love of sin, reliance on works, and our former opinions, habits, and passions. Most significantly, what we loved has passed away, especially the supreme love of self and with-it self-righteousness, self-promotion, and self-justification. The new creature looks outwardly toward Christ instead of inwardly toward self. The old things died, nailed to the cross with our sin nature.

Along with the old passing away, "the new has come!" Old, dead things are replaced with new things, full of life and the glory of God. The newborn soul delights in the things of God and abhors the things of the world and the flesh. Our purposes, feelings, desires, and understandings are fresh and different. We see the world differently.

The Bible seems to be a new book, and though we may have read it before, there is a beauty about it which we never saw before, and which we wonder at not having perceived. The whole face of nature seems to us to be changed, and we seem to be in a new world. The heavens and the earth are filled with new wonders, and all things seem now to speak forth the praises of God. There are new feelings toward all people—a new kind of love toward family and friends, a new compassion never before felt for enemies, and a new love for all mankind.

The things we once loved, we now detest. The sin we once held onto, we now desire to put away forever. We "put off the old man with his deeds" (Colossians 3:9), and put on the "New Man", created to be like God in true righteousness and holiness. (Ephesians 4:24).

What about the Christian who continues to sin? There is a difference between continuing to sin and continuing to live in sin. No one reaches sinless perfection in this life, but the redeemed Christian is being sanctified (made holy) day by day, sinning less and hating it more each time he fails. Yes, we still sin, but unwillingly and less and less frequently as we mature.

Our new self hates the sin that still has a hold on us. The difference is that the new creation is no longer a slave to sin, as we formerly were. We are now freed from sin and it no longer has power over us (Romans 6:6-7). Now we are empowered by and for righteousness. We now have the choice to "let sin reign" or to count ourselves "dead to sin but alive to God in Christ Jesus" (Romans 6:11-12). Best of all, now we have the power to choose the latter.

The new creation is a wondrous thing, formed in the

mind of God and created by his power and for his glory. (Excerpts for www.gotquestions.org)

I can testify to all the statements made here about this new creature. When I was "Born Again" I began to experience many of the changes that were discussed. I saw the world in a different light. It came alive in nature as never before.

When I read the Bible, key truths jumped off the pages into my heart. My attitudes slowly began to change for the better. My outlook on life went from depressed to positive. For the first time, I felt good about being alive. I had hope and felt loved by God. I suddenly became purpose driven.

It has been over 60 years since that "New Birth" experience. I have fallen, got back up, given up and pushed forward over the years but I am still kicking and still walking by faith with the Lord.

CONCLUSION

I certainly recommend being "Born Again" to all my readers. It was and still is the best thing that ever happened to me. I can see through the eyes of God and feel his heartbeat. I am privileged to know his thoughts on some things and to take part in his divine will. I have purpose in my life and a destiny to achieve.

I must tell you, for your own good, that the end goal of being "Born Again" is to be Christ-like. It is not to follow your own will but to do his will and be his ambassador in this world. If you are not sure of his will for you, listen to this:

"And God said, Let us make man in our image, after our likeness: and let them have dominion over the fish of the sea, and over the fowl of the air, and over the cattle, and over all the earth, and over every creeping thing that creepeth upon the earth. So God created man in his own image, in the image of God created he him; male and female created he them. Genesis 1:26-27" This is God's will. It was so from the beginning and it still is.

We are to be in reflection of God in the earth. His life and character are to flow from us. It is our divine destiny to be like him. If you do not know what the image and likeness is, read Galatian, chapter five about the fruit of the Spirit. You will see: Love, Joy, Peace, Longsuffering, and a lot of other goodness that is supposed to flow from God through you to reveal Christ on the earth. This is why we are "Born Again".

I hope you will take away these truths as you go on with your life:

- Being "Born Again" is a spiritual transformation that occurs when a person embraces faith in Jesus Christ.

- Being "Born Again" creates a "New Creature" that is created after God in true righteousness and holiness.

- Being "Born Again" causes old things to pass away and all things become new.

- Being "Born Again" can also be translated as "Born From Above." This can be likened to an overshadowing of the Holy Spirit as in the virgin birth of Mary. Every believer has their own virgin birth.

- Being "Born Again" makes us, no longer strangers, and aliens in this world but fellow citizens with the saints and a dwelling place (Temple) of God in the Spirit.

- Being "Born Again" can only happen through Jesus, The Christ. "Neither is there salvation in any other: for there is none other name under heaven given among men, whereby we must be saved." Acts 4:2

- Being "Born Again" is not a mere ritual; it is a profound transformation of the heart and soul. It is an invitation to experience God's grace and enter a new life in Christ.

- Being "Born Again" is being a "Butterfly" to soar on the wings of faith with God.

SELECTED CHRISTIAN POETRY BY JOHN MARINELLI, THE AUTHOR

"I AM" There

"**I AM**" There,
At the end of your broken dreams,
Before the sun rises over your day,
Prior to those tear-filled streams.

"**I AM**" There,
Down that road of despair,
When all appears to be lost,
And no one seems to care.

"**I AM**" There,
Over all of life's twists and turns,
When tomorrow is all but gone,
And when you are full of concerns.

"**I AM**" There,
Sayeth the Lord of Host,
To bring you hope and peace,
And the power of my Holy Ghost.

"**I AM**" There,
To be sure you make it through,
In the midst of every trial,
To bless your life and deliver you.

"I Am" There

"All power is given unto me in heaven and earth. Go ye therefore and teach all nations, baptizing them in the name of the Father, and of the Son, and of the Holy Ghost: Teaching them to observe all things, whatsoever I have commanded you: and lo, I am with you always, even unto the end of the world." Mathew 28:18-20

The Lord is with us always. He never leaves our side, even when we leave His. In every situation, He is there. It's time to count on His presence and trust in His grace.

Guardian Angel

The Angel of the Lord
Comes with a mighty army,
To fight the enemies of God.

Then he opens our eyes
That we might see the battle
And walk where angels trod.

Our guardian angels
Beholds the very face of God,
Standing there on our behalf.

Our guardian angels
Are ready with God's power,
To quiet evil's awful wrath.

"Take heed that ye despise not one of these little ones; for I say unto you, That in heaven, there angels do always behold the face of my Father, which is in heaven" Mathew 18:10

As God's children, we have guardian angels that watch over us and report back to God. They are ministering spirits especially placed in service to help the saints on their way to glory.

The Angel's Camp

The angel of the Lord
Sets up his camp
Around those that reverence God.

Imagine being there
In the midst of
Where angels trod.

What a joy it is
To know God's protection
And to be in the angel's camp.

It is there that God's children
Are delivered from evil's woe
And led by heaven's lamp.

"The angel of the Lord encamps round about them that fear Him, and delivers them" Psalm 34:7

Deliverance come through reverence and respect for God and a belief that He will be there with His angels to help you in times of trouble.

All Creation Waits

A blue-gray sky
Winks at the dawn,
As the morning light
Sings its glorious song.

Life is flourishing everywhere,
Unaware of what's in store.
The sounds of spring beckons,
In a silent and peaceful roar.

Time marches onward,
Towards the brink of day,
As all of creation waits
For God's children to pray.

It's time to stand up and be counted as a child of God. It's time to pray for peace and deliverance. Creation is waiting.

Don't Worry

Don't worry about tomorrow.
You did that yesterday.
Go on with your life
And remember always to pray.

Ask and it shall be given to you,
But this great truth you already know.
Rejoice and be happy, why? Because…
Your harvest comes from what you sow.

I will say it again and even more,
Until it becomes very very clear.
Tomorrow will take care of itself,
But worry is another word for fear.

Now here's what I want you to do.
Trust in the Lord and be of good cheer.
Drop the worry from your vocabulary
And cast out that demon of fear.

Worry is a sin so stop it. Be of good cheer. It's all up to you. Life is too short to spend it worrying.

Arm's Length

I hold the world at arm's length,
That its choices do not interfere.
While it does its own thing,
I watch and wait over here.

My steps must not go that way,
For it's not where I need to be.
The Lord has shown me the path,
That will lead me to my destiny.

The call to follow sin is strong
And pulls at me now and then.
But I know that way
Is full of sorrow and sin.

I must move on in life
Beyond their beckoning call.
It's the right thing to do,
So I do not stumble or fall.

I will not be swayed or misled
By family, friends or business deal.
Their secret thoughts are not mine,
To consider, to admire or feel.
So I keep the world at "Arm's Length"
As I journey through this life.
My faith in Jesus keeps me strong,
As I walk in His glorious light.

Arm's length is a good policy. Be sure you stay in the Lord and close to Him. It's the only way to keep sane in such a crazy world.

Clutter

Clutter keeps the mind confused,
As images dance through the night.
Lost among those unimportant thoughts,
Are the dreams that once shined bright.

An endless parade of fear and doubt,
Crowds the mind to destroy our day.
Ever soaring on the wings of the soul,
Until it has formed an evil array.

But clutter is by one's choice,
Of those who dance to its beat.
Better to face imaginations' due
Than to fall into utter defeat.

Set up a filter that keeps out unnecessary thoughts. A good practice is to go by the still waters in your mind and rest there until the flow of life situations becomes manageable.

I Find Myself In God

I find myself in God.
He is my "everything"
I know that He is Lord,
My Life, my Hope, and King.

I find myself in God,
Not the ways of sin.
Nor do I look to others,
To know who I really am.

I find myself in God,
To whom I bow on bended knee.
He alone is my joy and strength
And where I want to be.

You cannot really know yourself unless you first know God. He created you in His images and until you discover Him, you will never find yourself.

The Angels Cry "Holy,"

The Angels cry "Holy,"
While sorrow fills the land.
For God's Judgment Day,
Is to come upon every man.

The Angels cry "Holy,"
While mankind goes astray,
Rejecting the love of God,
To follow his own precarious way.

The Angels cry "Holy,"
Knowing the terror of the Lord,
When all who dwell in sin,
Will suddenly be destroyed.

The Angels cry "Holy,"
Waiting for all things new,
Born of the Holy Spirit,
When God's Judgment is through.

The Angels cry "Holy,"
"Holy is the Lamb,"
Waiting for the children of God,
To join "The Great I AM"

Heaven is waiting for us to join our Savior. What a great day that will be. Are you ready? I am.

Rest My Child

Take your peace and be restored
Then put your faith in Jesus, the Lord
He has provided, your mouth to feed.
From the beginning, He knew your need.

Do not worry, fret or even fear,
for, my child, He is always near.
To bless your soul with love and grace,
To be with you, face to face.

Come, my child, near to His throne.
Do not allow your faith to roam.
For those who will not believe,
Can never find rest in times of need.

His word shall see you through.
His grace He freely gives to you.
That you should rest, your soul to keep,
Forever delivered from unbelief.

Go ahead, rest in the Lord. I dare you. It may be scary at first but it sure feels good when you get use to it.

Winning The Battle

We must use the Word of God
To calm emotions that fray.
For the enemy never sleeps,
Until he has led us astray.

So when your emotions overflow
With feelings like depression and fear.
Know this! If you dwell in that place,
You invite the enemy to draw near.

When your emotions rage
With fiery darts aglow,
Stand in the power of the Lord,
Against its awful woe.

And if you get confused
And lost in the storm,
Put your thoughts on trial,
Rejecting all but heaven born.

You can win the battle
That rages within your soul.
By casting down imaginations,
And breaking Satan's hold.
Remember to focus on Jesus,
Holding the world at arm's length.
Lift up your head above the trial,
And the Lord will give you strength.

"For the weapons of our warfare are not carnal but mighty, through God, to the pulling down of strongholds: casting down imaginations and every high thing that exalts itself against the knowledge of God, and bringing into captivity every thought to the obedience of Christ." II Corinthians 10:3-5 The battle is in our minds and we win by putting our thoughts on trial and casting out all that oppose the knowledge of God. This is true victory.

Little Prisons

Little prisons await the man with a lustful soul.
Bars of selfishness and pride create dungeons of icy cold.

Prisons of shame and jealousy fill
the heart with utter despair.
Bars that separate from God and those that really care.

Stand back! While the doors are tightly closed;
Taking away your life, to wither as a dying rose.

Beware of those little prisons that trap the lustful soul.
Keep yourself free from sin through
faith in the Christ of old.

Little prisons need not to be your fate.
It is your choice, Spirit or flesh to date.

"O Foolish Galatians, who hath bewitched you, that ye should not obey the truth, before whose eyes Jesus Christ hath been, evidently set forth, crucified among you? Are you so foolish? Having begun in the Spirit, are you now made perfect in the flesh?

We should always seek to dwell in the Spirit, that we would not emulate the deeds of the flesh. When we fall short, we create "little prisons" that keep us in confusion and away from the blessing of God. It's time to walk in the Spirit and break the prisons that so easily beset us.

The Wrestling Match

We wrestle not with flesh and blood,
For man is not our enemy.
Instead, we fight demons in the spirit
That seek to steal our destiny.

But our weapons are not earthly,
Like tanks, guns or bombs.
Instead, we "Plead The Blood"
And shout our victory songs.

So do not wrestle with humanity
Even though evil is there.
Go after Satan, the real enemy
And strip his kingdom bare.

"For though we walk in the flesh, we do not war after the flesh: for the weapons of our warfare are not carnal but mighty, through God, to the pulling down of strongholds; casting down imaginations and every high thing that exalts itself above the knowledge of God, and bring into captivity, every thought to the obedience of Christ." II Corinthians 10: 3-6

Don't fight with other people. Just go about your own business, counting on God to be the avenger. He is the one that holds all the power and strength. If we fight in the flesh, we can fall to strongholds and demons. But standing up in the Spirit and using the name of Jesus, applying the knowledge of God in the situation and casting down every ungodly imagination, will always lead us to victory.

Oh' The Blood

Oh, the blood of Jesus
That washed away my sin.
What a great blessing
To have God as my friend.

This one thing I know for sure,
That when I confess my sin,
His cleansing blood will flow,
And I can walk again with Him.

Oh, the blood of Jesus,
How great a sacrifice for me.
For it was the blood of the Lamb
That healed my soul and set me free.

"If we confess our sins, he is faithful and just to forgive us our sins and to cleanse us from all unrighteousness." I John 1:9

It is the blood of Jesus that is the cleansing agent in forgiveness, acceptance by God and salvation of the soul. Without His blood, there would be no payment for sin. Saint John, in chapter three, says that the wages for sin is death. Jesus paid the price so we could go free to serve God, the Father.

One Man

It was by one man, Adam,
That the world fell into sin.
He chose to disobey God's word
And lost God's Spirit within.

No more walks with God
Through the garden of God's grace.
No more close up and personal
To walk along and talk, face to face.

One man, Adam, gave up
The very nature of God.
Never again to stroll along
Where angels once trod.

Evil now flows through his blood
Where only righteousness was before.
He gave up the Spirit of life
To open up death's awful door.

But one Man, Jesus, came from God
To seek and to save that which was lost.
The life of God in man, once again,
Because He paid sin's incredible cost.

"Therefore, as by one man, sin entered into the world, and death by sin; and so death passed upon all men, for that all have sinned. For as by one man's disobedience, many were made sinners, so by the obedience of one, many shall be made righteous." Romans 5:12 & 19

Adam fell and lost the Spirit of God inside of him because of his disobedience; But Jesus obeyed, did not fall and restored what Adam lost. All die in Adam because of sin but all who believe in Jesus shall live in Christ because of His righteousness.

In The Fullness of Time

In the fullness of time,
Jesus came, made of a woman.
Our Heavenly Father sent Him
Because our adoption was at hand.

He was born under the law,
So He might redeem us from it,
And to receive adoption as sons,
Being children of God, we sit.

We who God made His children,
Have the Spirit of His Son,
Deep within our heart of hearts,
So we can finally become one.

"But when the fullness of time was come, God sent forth his son, made of a woman, made under the law, to redeem them that were under the law, that we might receive the adoption of sons. And because we are sons, God has sent forth the spirit of his son into our hearts, crying, Abba, Father." Galatians 4:4-6

We are the adopted sons of God. We, like no other, have the indwelling presence of the Spirit of His Son, who cries out unto God the Father. If your spirit is not crying out to God, you may want to find out why?

Fragile Flower Red

As a flower in earthen sod,
I bloom for thee, oh God.
To blossom with the turn of spring;
To be to you, a beautiful thing.

I lift my Fragile Flower Red
Upward from my earthen bed;
To draw light from God above,
Strength and peace and joy and love.

As a flower, I bloom for thee
That passersby may stop and see.
Your fragrance and beauty I am,
Flowered in grace as a man.

As a flower in earthen sod,
I bloom for thee, oh God.
Upward, I lift my head,
As a Fragile Flower Red.

"Be not conformed to this world, but be ye transformed, by the renewing of your mind, that ye may prove what is that good and acceptable and perfect will of God."

When we look to God as our source, we blossom, much like a flower that draws light from the sun. When we blossom, like a flower, we display the glory and beauty of our creator to all who care to stop and look. This is our divine providence.

ABOUT THE AUTHOR

Rev. Marinelli is an ordained minister, He has formed and been pastor of one church in Wisconsin and was the pastor of another in Alabama. He has also been a youth minister and evangelism director over the years.

Rev. Marinelli has authored over 30-books that can be viewed on his website:

www.marrinellichristianbooks.com

John is an accomplished Christian poet. He also dabbles in songwriting and writing one act Christian plays. He is the Vice President of Have A Heart For Companion Animals, Inc., a "No Kill" animal welfare organization.

He volunteers his time promoting fundraising events for
www.haveaheartusa.org.

Rev. Marinelli is now retired from the sales and marketing
arena after spending over 40 years in business-to-business
and non-profit marketing. He enjoys writing Christian
themed books, playing chess, singing karaoke and a retired lifestyle in sunny Florida

For More Info eMail Contact:

johnmarinelli@embarqmail.com